Then & Now
GUERNSEY

Then & Now
GUERNSEY

PATRICIA & BRIAN SHIPMAN

TEMPUS

Frontispiece: A visit to Guernsey is always a celebration. This unknown photograph from the turn of the twentieth century is celebrating an unknown event, or perhaps from today's viewpoint it is celebrating Guernsey for all that is offered to resident and visitor alike.

First published 2004

Tempus Publishing Limited
The Mill, Brimscombe Port,
Stroud, Gloucestershire, GL5 2QG
www.tempus-publishing.com

© Patricia & Brian Shipman, 2004

The right of Patricia & Brian Shipman to be identified as the Author of this work has been asserted in accordance with the Copyrights, Designs and Patents Act 1988.

All rights reserved. No part of this book may be reprinted or reproduced or utilised in any form or by any electronic, mechanical or other means, now known or hereafter invented, including photocopying and recording, or in any information storage or retrieval system, without the permission in writing from the Publishers.

British Library Cataloguing in Publication Data.
A catalogue record for this book is available from the British Library.

ISBN 0 7524 3310 5

Typesetting and origination by Tempus Publishing Limited
Printed in Great Britain

CONTENTS

Acknowledgements 6

Introduction 7

1.   Arrival in Guernsey 9

2.   The Town of St Peter Port 27

3.   Beyond the Town 51

4.   People, Places and Puzzles 81

ACKNOWLEDGEMENTS

We would like to thank the people of Guernsey who, by their enthusiasm, encouraged the completion of this book: The Priaulx Library, particularly Mr Riccy Allen for his patience and knowledge; The Guernsey Museum; Mr Ebenezer Le Page – a famous Guernsey man who never drew a breath. It is wrong to say he never lived because he lives on every page of the book by the late G.B. Edwards: *Illustrated Guide to, and Popular History of the Channel Islands of 1880*. Finally to all the cousins we found on the island that encouraged and helped us immensely.

INTRODUCTION

The story of how this book came into being goes back many years. The Ozanne family line goes back to the days when Queen Elizabeth, eager to retain her Normandy outposts, peopled the island with settlers. They were given incentives to go there and more to stay. Full histories of Guernsey abound and the interested enquirer is referred to Guernsey Museum or The Priaulx Library. These can be found next to each other in Candie Gardens, which can be entered by foot from St Julian's Avenue at the junction with Candie Road at St Peter Port.

The Ozanne family still have deeds to a property called Les Landes (Les Landes du marché) which was acquired by the family in 1576. Before that the history can be traced to back to the exotic Andros family (this name comes from the Andrews family in Northampton who were among the early settlers planted in Guernsey by Queen Elizabeth to create an English heritage). Along the related Collings line, records amazingly go back as far as AD 406. Among other things they sailed the seas and were granted Letters of Marque or privateering papers against the French. The exceedingly testing waters around the island would always provide the able and knowledgeable seaman with a living one way or another. There have always been close connections with the French whether with trading or fighting or breeding. The family comes down through the ages with strong connections to many other Channel island families, interweaving a complex pattern to make up the fabric of the people of Channel Islands today. Almost any Guernsey family of the early period of this book could find a relationship with every other family either on Guernsey, Jersey or any of the other islands if they looked hard enough.

The period covered in this volume involves four generations of one family. Jean Le Patourel (1810–1898), a businessman; his daughter Elizabeth (1835–1929), who married local Law Agent Alfred Guerin; their daughter Alice Rose (1855–1929), who married a young clergyman Richard Edwyn Ozanne and was widowed at the age of twenty-nine; Catherine May (1881–1963), Alice's daughter who married Harold Hamilton, a stranger to the island, and subsequently left for England. She was widowed at the age of thirty-seven. Neither widow married again.

Photography was probably an expensive hobby so the family were not short of money or leisure time. Possibly they processed their own photographs as well as collected other prints etc. of the time. Who took the actual photographs is not certain. Perhaps several members of the family did.

In around 1990 Patricia Shipman, the author, and granddaughter of Catherine May Ozanne, was given a collection of old glass negative plates that had lain in the cellar of the family house in Chiswick, London, for seventy years. Having an interest in photography she determined to make prints from these plates despite the fact that they were in very poor condition. This book is largely produced from that collection. Other pictures used are from the family collection.

Unusually, a lot of these photographs are casual or even un-posed – often without the photographer seemingly being noticed. All the better for that. They show the people and places that the family knew and loved. They reveal that the Victorians were just as capable of enjoying themselves as any other age. It is a pity that we do not know all the names of the people in the photographs.

Having printed the old glass slides, a visit was then made to the island with the prints. Local people spoken to were very interested, and it was decided to try and revisit the sites to see how things had changed. A most enjoyable two weeks were then spent on this. The production of the box of prints in a restaurant or public house was enough to gather a crowd around the table and suggestions flew thick and fast.

Without the help of the local people the book would never have come to pass. Without the encouragement of Guernsey Museum, who greatly enjoyed seeing the photographs, and without BBC Radio Guernsey who interviewed Patricia, the job would not have been finished.

The Victorian visitor could buy a ticket from Southampton to St Peter Port. The Great Western Railway owned the ferries but there is no known railway on the island. The visitors would have had a voyage that they would remember. The old ferries were far from slow even by today's standards. A single fare cost 33 shillings first class; 23 shillings second class or 20 shillings third class. Return tickets cost 48 shillings first class, 38 shilling second class and 30 shillings for third class. There were also various offers and deals as there are today. So says the 1880 guide.

The island itself covers an area of twenty-four square miles. It is divided into ten parishes, most still bearing their old French names. The island still retains much of the old Norman system of laws.

The reader may like to consider that he or she is being taken on a personal tour of the island by islanders who lived more than 100 years ago. There is much more of interest that is not even mentioned, being outside the scope of this book. Some of the island's most memorable history had not happened yet. By following the route in the book the reader will soon be diverted to other things, but the book is there to come back to. By the end a lot of extra pleasure, it is hoped, will be gained.

Finally we apologise for any errors that may become apparent. A lot of stories and memories have changed over time and a number of photographs, for example Doyle Column have been included more for pleasure than historical accuracy.

Chapter 1

ARRIVAL IN GUERNSEY

For the visitor to Guernsey, for most of its history, arrival would have been by ship. The first glimpse you will have on approach to the island is the town of St Peter Port. Names like the 'Race of Alderney' and the 'Little Russel' mean little to the modern visitor, but in the days before radar and modern navigational aid could cut through the mist the sailor needed be very aware that the sea was not his friend. With tidal ranges that can exceed nine meters, the hard granite rocks and islets appear and disappear all around the island. These dangers protected the island from the stranger as much as they were a danger to the unwary. The mariner from the past was truly grateful when he could tie up to that solid granite and come ashore on what is without doubt one of the finest jewels of the British Isles. Its history goes far, far back before Roman times when it was called 'Sarnia'; a name that still has echoes around the island. So many things from the past are preserved and cherished that it could be said that history can be tripped over at every step.

Here is one of the fleet of steamers that would have brought a visitor through the tricky waters to Guernsey without the benefit of modern aids. This ferry, entering the harbour at the turn of the twentieth century, was photographed from the end of White Rocks Pier. It was capable of completing the journey from Weymouth in four hours and twenty minutes. There was considerable competition between the various ferries. Today the modern vessel manages the same journey in just two and a half hours.

The point where the old photograph was taken is just beyond the barrier. Not much has changed in the modern photograph, although a more modern lighthouse has been installed at the end of Castle Pier and it seems smaller. In the past the comings and goings of ships would have been of great interest to the local people, who would perhaps stand for hours to glimpse an important visitor coming to the island.

On this occasion there are quite a few people waiting for what looks like the same ferry to moor upon the opposite side of the pier. It is surprising how small these plucky vessels were when compared with today's large modern ferries. Above all they were designed for speed and The Great Western Railway had the latest and fastest designs.

In the modern view the slipway on the other side of the port looks exactly as before, though there are now more buildings on Castle Pier and also visible are the masts of modern yachts, which are more easily be lifted out of the water. There are also more trees now on the hill behind Havelet Bay. There will be more information on the ships that served the people of Guernsey at the end of our tour when we return again to the port area.

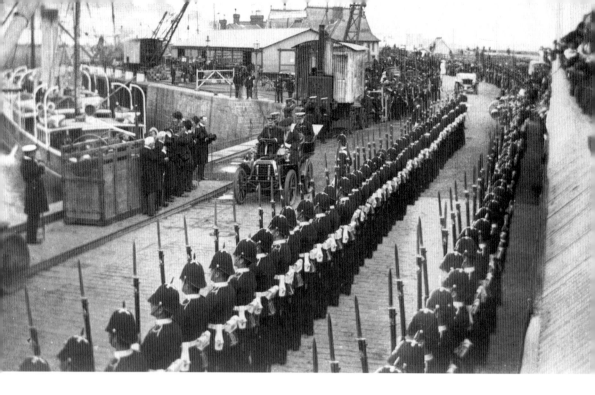

Looking towards St Julian's Pier. Perhaps the crowd in the previous photograph would also have lined the wall to see more of this dignitary. It has been suggested that he might be Arthur, the Duke of Connaught, said to be Queen Victoria's favourite son, who made a visit in 1905 at about the time this photograph was taken. If so then it is just before 9 a.m. on Tuesday 26 September 1905. The guard of honour comprised 100 men of the 13th Company the Royal Garrison Artillery and the 2nd Battalion of the Manchester Regiment.

The obvious contrast between the two photographs is the sight of new docks and buildings which were not there at the beginning of the twentieth century. The construction of the modern quay – still described as 'new' – is far less elegant than the old stonework, although in the modern photograph the stone dock behind the approaching car still has the steps leading down to the sea, seen painted white between the legs of the great modern crane. It is interesting to see that the rail along which the old crane ran is still visible on the edge of the dock. Even larger cranes now crowd the dock to handle the increase in freight.

The great man has left his car and, whilst courtesies are exchanged, at least one of the party is caught mopping his brow. Just beyond the head of the harassed dignitary a buoy sits in the harbour, and beyond numerous boats lie at moorings which are now covered by the new buildings. But for this the background slopes of the town have changed very little. The walkway from which these photographs were taken is still accessible on foot.

This is exactly the same area as the previous two pages, except now the port is back to work. The baskets were used for carrying tomatoes, for which the island was famous, and were returnable for re-use. Cargo of all types is piled up along the port ready for lifting aboard with the cranes.

These may have been steam-powered, as what appears to be steam can be seen emitting from the corrugated iron roof. Between the cranes are the hand barrows which would be piled high with luggage and goods for moving around the port. The horse in his own cradle awaits loading, although it is of course possible that he has just been offloaded. Horse racing took place on the island at L'Ancresse. Gas lighting indicates that the port may well be working both night and day. The bar on the side of the gas lamp enabled a ladder to be placed alongside it for maintenance work on the lamp. Gas is no longer used on the island. The modern quay shows the massive cranes now in use, and the slipway in the background.

The fresh produce ready for shipment was laid out without the benefit of modern storage facilities. The produce was transferred to the port from the farms and vineries ready for the vessels, which were more strictly under the control of tidal conditions than modern vessels. Here can be seen tomato baskets and barrels for salted fish. The Channel current sweeps down between the islands at a very high speed through the Race of Alderney. The ships, with their limited power, would need to come down with the current and load up quickly ready to leave with the return current, or wait for the next tide. To consider the option of fighting the current would probably be out of the question on the grounds of cost and time. Even the most modern of ferries at this time would be extremely limited in their power, unlike their modern counterpart, to which the current is barely a factor.

The building in the old view was demolished in the 1930s and the area developed into a loading area for cars using the modern ferries. This photograph was taken from the walkway which goes to the end of White Rock Pier. We will return to this location in the last chapter.

This is the Albert Pier as it would have appeared if you were to stand with your back to the town. The photograph was taken between 1890 and 1900. Rising up in the distance on the right is Castle Cornet. This was where freight such as coal arrived from areas of mainland Britain such as Shields, Swansea, Glasgow, Llanelli, Hull, Grimsby, Burryport, Newcastle and Goole. The passenger ferries were very competitive with each other but the more leisured requirements of freight meant that older and slower ships were still in use.

It is surprising to see that the seats on top of the buildings at the end of the pier are still in place, as are the bollards. The motor car makes its presence felt and takes up a large area, which the far-sighted planners allowed for when the port was enlarged at a cost of £350,000 (before 1880). The foundation stone for the new harbour was laid in around 1853, but that was just the beginning of many years of hard work.

This old print shows the plaque commemorating Queen Victoria's arrival to Guernsey on 24 August 1846, which is still to be seen. It offers a better view along the quayside. The stone is still in place and the slip is used for access to the drying hard. Vessels such as these shown here would ground onto the hard when the tide dropped, taking the water from the harbour. It can be seen in the modern view that the ledge built to support the coal barges at the Quay still serve a useful purpose; supporting visiting yachts when it is necessary for them to be inspected below the water line. Some sailors take this opportunity to give the underside of their vessels a quick coat of paint or to clean off the accumulated weed.

A few paces further along the Quay is this view towards North Esplanade and the start of Victoria Pier, also known as Crown Pier. It will take a sharp eye to find many differences in the buildings along the Quay. Today the character of the area remains the same and it is to hoped that Albert and Victoria would not be disapprove too much. The yachts in the marina have left for their winter quarters though flowers still bloom in Guernsey's temperate climate. The statue of Prince Albert was, according to an 1880 guidebook, built by public subscription and unveiled in October 1863, and was a copy of an original by Joseph Durham A.R.A. which was designed to be placed in the Horticultural Gardens of South Kensington.

View from Castle Pier looking towards the town. The summer foliage of the trees hides the bulk of St Peter Port Church. A modern freighter is aground against the Town Wall and the steam yacht, also aground, is moored to Crown Pier.

The modern photograph also shows the trees at the bus depot in front of the church but a few of the buildings seem much changed. The large number of yachts moored to the pontoons reflects the changing use of the harbour and the crowded nature of the area today. A bar at the marina entrance now keeps the water level up. Visiting yachts from ports in Britain and Europe can often be seen and occasionally boats from further away, such as America or Australia. Guernsey is a haven for both the traveller and the holidaymaker.

Taken almost at the same spot on Albert Pier as the previous view, this photograph could also have been taken at around the same time as the bowsprit of a sailing vessel appears in both. However, whereas the picture on the previous page shows a relaxed aspect one could suppose was a quiet Sunday, this one could well have been taken on a Monday morning as people go about their day-to-day work. The frontages of the present buildings present a less jumbled aspect.

On the opposite side of Albert Pier, Alice Rose Ozanne looks towards Castle Cornet in the distance. To the right of it is the slip which appears on page eleven. In the modern photograph Patricia Shipman, author and great granddaughter of Alice Rose, can see a new wall and harbour gate at Fish Quay between the pier and the slip. But essentially Albert Pier remains as it always has been, even to the extent of being able to identify the actual paving stones Alice trod on.

The old picture, showing the area between the Castle Pier and Albert Pier, was taken after 1863 as the Albert statue is visible. It was taken at the point on Castle Pier where the new Fish Quay begins. The new Fish Quay was completed in 1989 and cost £1.4 million. It makes no pretensions to beauty and in that respect does not disappoint.

With the town now behind us we can begin the walk along the Castle Pier that leads out to Castle Cornet. Once the castle was on an island and this road was built for obvious reasons in 1869. The road is freely accessible on foot and leads to the castle which has many attractions to the visitor, including a portrait of Richard Mansell Ozanne, grandfather of Alice Rose's husband Richard Edwin Ozanne, and storekeeper and barrack master to the garrison in the castle for forty-seven years. He died in 1866, the same year the lighthouse at the end of the Castle Pier was built (though it was commissioned in 1867). In the distance appears a battleship and the people around the car could well be in uniform. Perhaps this group are part of the VIP visitors seen at the beginning of our tour.

Today this road along the pier has changed less than the castle – which seems to have lost a building and a chimneystack – though the road is no longer open for general use by vehicles.

Further along South Esplanade we come to what was, until recently, the Guernsey Brewery. This was started by Jean Le Patourel in 1845 and grew into the present building by about 1858. His name is on a lintel in Havelet at the side of the brewery where he also lived. He was the paternal grandfather of Alice Rose Ozanne and appears in family photographs later in this book. From this and other breweries beer would have been taken by road using horse-drawn carriages such as those shown in the photographs.

The modern photograph was taken in 1995 shortly before brewing ceased. The building is now empty and various ideas have been put forward for its use. Most people hope that the façade will be preserved. Sadly the dray has gone.

This view along Havelet shows the house, known as Les Terres, which possibly pre-dates the completed brewery. Jean Le Patourel, known to many as 'Grandpere Les Terres', was an extremely successful businessman and oversaw the growth of the brewery building from little more than a kiln in 1845; drawing water from the two valleys adjacent to the land he secured. Much of this land was incorporated into the major improvements completed during this period to the port and South Esplanade. Le Patourel named the brewery 'The London Brewery' and while there is no doubt that there was a very good reason for this, it is now lost to us. Land, for which he had paid £35 was sufficient for the project, which was completed by 1863. Jean Le Patourel died at Les Terres on 26 January 1898, aged eighty-eight years.

This modern photograph shows that the height of the wall has been increased where La Valette begins, and Le Val de Terre begins its climb out of the town.

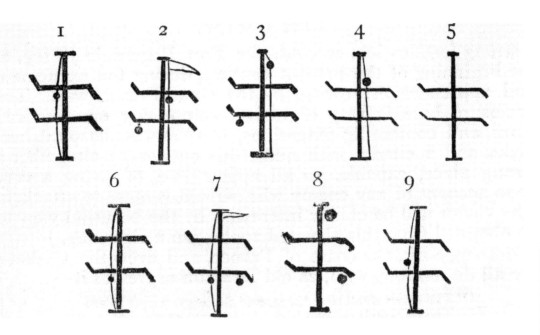

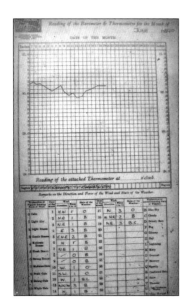

O nce more we are indebted to the 1880 guide for this information. The signs mean as follows: 1. Packet due from England; 2. Packet still due from England, but a steamer in sight; 3. Packet from England in sight; 4. Packet from England in the harbour; 5. Packet arrived and proceeded; 6. Packet due from Jersey; 7. Packet still due from Jersey, but a steamer in sight; 8. Packet from Jersey in sight; 9. Packet from Jersey in the harbour. It was important to know when ships were due. In the days before refrigeration, produce had to come from farms at the very last minute in order to preserve freshness. We may have more modern ways now but for sheer simplicity and ingenuity the Victorians can teach us much.

On the left is the weather trend for the month prior to 19 June 1940, which can be found in the side window of the Piquet House on the corner of Church Hill. The practice ceased on that day which was the beginning of the Occupation. The Piquet House, built in 1819 was a guardhouse from where they sent the guard to Government House. There was a strong room at the opposite end of the building for disorderly persons.

Chapter 2

THE TOWN OF ST PETER PORT

This illustration of the Parish Church, St Peter Port, in around 1860 is from *Ward & Lock's Illustrated Guide to and history of The Channel Islands* published in about 1880, when so many of the improvements to create the Town and Port we know today were still being completed. It gives us a good idea of how much the old has been incorporated with the new on the island. The Parish Church, or Town Church, was said to have been completed in 1312 in granite brought from France. The *Illustrated Guide* says that it did not escape 'renovation in the churchwarden style' in 1812. A charter of William of Normandy confirmed patronage of the church to the Abbey of Marmontier, near Tours in France, in 1065 by William, who then went on to conquer England. This view of the church is from the beginning of Fountain Street and is, of course, St Peter's. It is the senior church of the island and the Rector from 1870 to 1881 was Richard James Ozanne, the great, great, grandfather of the author. The Dean of Guernsey would also have been at this church and may also have been the Rector. The island lies within the diocese of Winchester.

Looking south down the High Street this scene, again from Ward & Lock's 1880 guide, must be from an even earlier period. It says: 'If the old town consists of narrow streets and lanes, more suggestive of mediaeval picturesque-ness than comfort and convenience, there is, on the other hand plenty of evidence of the spirit of modern improvement.'

The guide mentions that wines and spirits are generally cheaper than in England, especially the latter, on account of the absence of any but trifling excise duties. It also mentions that purchase with English money is favourable and that French money is legal tender. Parts of St Peter Port in the older image have not changed; they are seen in the modern photograph.

Under the heading of weights and measures, it says that the pound weight in Guernsey is heavier than the English to the extent of nearly 9 per cent.

Although the church is shown with reasonable accuracy, considerable changes appear in respect of the buildings. However one can still, in the words of the 1880 guide, 'perambulate steep and crooked streets, flanked by substantial but old dusky houses' and enjoy the varied attractions the town has to offer shoppers or tourists.

The French Market, also known as the French Hales, has always been of considerable significance in every sense when taken into account in the development of the town. Trade has always been conducted with France in both directions. Now small shops still trade within.

This old scene is taken from the doorway of the Town Market in Market Street – currently under the threat of redevelopment. The building of the Market was financed very cleverly. The story goes as follows: In 1820 the States agreed to build a covered market for £5,500. As they had £1,000 in hand, £4,500 in £1 notes was issued on the security of a small tax on spirituous liquor. The work was undertaken and the Market completed and opened in 1822. Each of the thirty-six shops yielded £5 in rent. As soon as the £180 was received each year, £180 State notes were burnt. The £4,500 notes would have taken too long to destroy at this rate but the States also paid into the Market Fund £300 per annum derived from tax on wines coming into the island. £30 of this was set aside for running repairs and £270 went towards the extinction of more paper notes. At the end of ten years not one of the notes issued to pay for the building was left, no interest had been paid upon them and there was a steady income of £180 per annum.

This is an example of one of the many stepped passageways and stairways that can be found all over the town of St Peter Port, which nestles against a hill. Those venturing up such a climb can often be rewarded with unexpected views of the town and the sea beyond. These steps run from Market Street, just beyond the French Hales, up to Clifton. Although this very early reproduction shows houses on both sides, the ones on the right have now disappeared. Those knowledgeable about the town and its shortcuts can use these passages to move quickly from one part of the town to another.

A few paces back along Market Street towards the town (with the French Market on your left) will bring you to the steps shown here. Previously the shop on the right-hand-side was owned by the Pay family. The Royal Crest on the shop in the centre was displayed in 1900 and the words 'By Appointment' displayed below. Note the clock on the first floor window, which can still be seen today above the jewellers. Today the maze of little streets nearby remains a busy shopping area. In both photographs the blinds are down against the sunshine, evidence of Guernsey's very temperate climate.

During the 1890s, just beside the Town Church in Church Square, the horse bus has arrived. This picture would be very different had the people been aware of the photographer – rare indeed is the unposed photograph from this period. Horse buses were gradually replaced in the early 1900s and a tram ran along the front at this time. Note the lady standing on the right with her cloak. Above her head appears to be a mirror, which can also be seen in the photograph on page 33.

Today No.1 Church Square still has its curved frontage and the curb line is the same. Over the years the businesses have changed hands, for example A.G. Quick has been replaced by Evelyn's; however Le Lievre's has long been established.

Note the 'mirror' at the top left-hand corner of the photograph below. In this view the people are climbing onto the horse bus. One is bound to wonder if the horse is expected to pull that load up the hills out of the town. The ivy-covered building is the rear of The Albion House Hotel. In days gone by cattle passed this way to and from the docks along what was once called Cow Lane. It is again amazing that no-one seems to have noticed the camera.

The blank wall behind the telephone boxes is the rear of the Albion today, now stripped of its ivy. On the right is the wall of the church. Cars have replaced the horses.

Part of the charm of St Peter Port are the little passageways and steps which act as shortcuts around the town and lead to places like Candie Gardens with its wonderful views out to sea. Here is Alice Rose Ozanne standing in Beauregard Lane at the back of La Fregate Hotel in around 1890. The gateway is now the entrance to the hotel car park. Sadly the gates are gone, though with them the entrance would be quite narrow for modern vehicles, as it was originally designed for the horse-drawn age.

Walk on along Beauregard Lane past the Museum and Art Gallery. At the end turn left and left again into Candie Road. The first on the right will take you into Arsenal Road and soon you will arrive at The Military Arsenal. It was used for keeping the guns and accoutrements, and clothing for the militia. Though most of the Royal Guernsey Militia was manned by volunteers they were trained to protect the island if ever necessary. On the day when the old photograph was taken the men are preparing for a special event, possibly the Chevauchée as they carry long poles like those used for measuring in this ceremony. The man on the horse directly behind the two militiamen appears again later.

Two canons, taken at Sebastopol during the Crimean war, were presented by Queen Victoria and placed on either side of the entrance to the drill ground. They are now in the grounds of the Victoria Tower opposite. During the Occupation they were buried as it was thought that they might be mistaken for artillery and be bombed. The Victoria Tower was built in red granite at a cost of more than £2,000 and was named after the Queen. It was intended to commemorate her visit with Prince Albert on 24 August 1846.

With the fire station on your right walk to the end of Arsenal Road and turn left into Brock Road. The house where Alice Rose lived is next door to the Ebenezer Chapel. It is not known when the house was built but it was called Lucknow, the name it bears to this day. Mrs Amelia Mauger, who was a relative by marriage to Jean Le Patourel, lived next door. The house was rented to Alice Rose Ozanne who was widowed at a very young age and never remarried. The property laws of Guernsey were, and still are, very complex. The large extended family relationships meant that a home would have been found for her and her four children. Alice would probably not have gone to the Ebeneezer Chapel as it was Methodist and she was the widow of an Anglican parson.

The church is currently not in use but there is hope that the structure will be saved and given another useful purpose. It can be seen that the present owners have carefully preserved the external features of the house.

This is the view from the first floor window of Lucknow looking across Brock Road. The horse on the left has a lady's side saddle and the one on the right a normal saddle. The washing on the line is on land which was, at the time this photograph was taken, part of Miller's livery stables, which appear in the following photographs. Alice Rose Ozanne lost her husband when he was thirty-six years old and she was twenty-eight. He died in South Shields but was brought home to Guernsey to be buried in the family vault. She was left with three sons and a daughter. She lived in this house until she left for England in around 1910.

The 'new' houses opposite Lucknow were built in the early 1900s, around the same time the motor car was having an impact on the livery business.

Another view from the first floor window of Lucknow. The wall of Miller's stables extends to the gate shown here. The two horsemen, seemingly in fancy dress, are quite possibly involved in a local pageant; an event which unfolds over the following pages.

Looking left towards the house that has now become St Clare Court Hotel, traces of the original building are evident around the front door and surrounding windows. The new extension to the original boundary is clear. The trees have grown up to obscure the house behind the high wall in the old photograph, which is one of the houses in Les Gravees, which will be seen on the next page. It is interesting to note that the pillars and the gate to Ebenezer Church have survived.

Lucknow can be seen beyond the Ebenezer Chapel on the right, as final preparations are being made for an event which might be La Chevauchée de St Michel. This ceremony was held in May and dates back to pagan rituals. Pions, young men wearing the magical colours of red, white and black, would process to certain heathen landmarks, eat in fairy circles and participate in ceremonies which can only be guessed at. To make things worse the pions had the right to kiss any woman they met on the way. There is little to suggest that the women hid away in horror. A similar celebration was held in France at Mont St Michel from which Abbey Christianity is believed to have later spread to the island. Over the years the pagan aspect was sublimated by the new order. The monks, appalled to find that public kissing of women was permitted on this occasion, no doubt wondered what that led to. However, on finding the local people were not disinclined to do away altogether with the ceremony, a compromise was found.

With the church on your left walk towards the main road and turn right. The event is now in full swing. A Guernsey militiaman can be seen in uniform in the picture. Note the decorated carriage seen on the previous page. The girl in the carriage on the right and the man at the back on the same side are the only people who appear to have noticed the camera. Perhaps we will meet them again later. It is probable that the whole of these series of photographs around the Brock Road area were taken around the same period, the first decade of the twentieth century, before the enormous hats of the pre-war period became fashionable.

The modern photograph shows the same junction at Grange Road, The Queens Road and Les Gravees. On the left, behind the trees, is the back of the house seen on page 36. Apart from 100 years of tree growth little seems to have changed in the house or the layout of the road. Gas lamps have been replaced by electric street lighting. The Guernsey filter system regulates traffic at this busy junction where main roads go off to the west and south of the island.

This is probably the same occasion, presumed to be La Chevauchée de St Michel. This scene is slightly turned to the right and looks down Grange Road towards the town centre. By the line of people on the right of the old scene it is difficult to imagine that the footway has changed much over the years. A chimney has been lost here and there. The first house on the left is at the beginning of Brock Road and it is interesting to see that it was not built upon even then.

The junction into Brock Road now has traffic lights and the little public garden can be seen. The 'filter' marked on the road is the same one seen on the previous page.

If we leave Brock Road to turn our attention to Grange Road, we go along Les Gravees, turn left at St Stephen's Church onto St Stephen's Hill, then via Les Croutes to Kings Road. About half way along on the right-hand-side is the entrance to Elizabeth College playing fields; in that road on the left is this special little house. At the turn of the twentieth century it was called Lloydminster.

Two of Catherine's brothers migrated to Lloydminster in Canada. This is where Alice Rose Ozanne's daughter, Catherine, lived after marrying Harold Hamilton in 1907, before the couple left the island to seek their fortune in England a year or two later. Possibly the reason the photograph was taken was due to the fact that it had been snowing, and thought unusual enough to justify marking the occasion.

It can be seen in the modern photograph that the cosy house has since been extended. During the Occupation Mr Bill (William John) Allen, groundsman of St Elizabeth's College for many years until 1967, lived here. In 1940 he bravely hid two young British Officers who were Guernsey men (and old Elizabethans) under the nearby pavilion and brought them home to this house to share his limited rations. He was arrested for his pains but later he was released and allowed to resume his duties.

The photograph at the top of this page shows Catherine May Ozanne at the rear of her new home in Kings Road just after her marriage on 26 December 1907 to Harold Hamilton. He was described on the marriage certificate as a photographer and his home as Stockport, Lancashire. So by then he might have given up the Moncrieffe Vinery which will be visited later in the book.

The couple were married at St Stephen's Church which displays an important series of stained glass windows designed by William Morris. While he was responsible for the overall design of his windows, for the actual scenes Morris employed various pre-Raphaelite artists including Dante Gabriel Rossetti, Philip Webb and Edward Burne-Jones.

The rear of Lloydminster in Kings Road, seen on the previous page. Now we can see the back of the house has not changed in appearance though it now boasts an extension.

From Kings Road via Ville au Roi and Les Preteaux to the beginning of Rue Poudreuse, a detour to the left down a straight lane will take you to the Ozanne Mill, built by a Mr James Ozanne in 1825. There is no evidence to connect him with the same branch of the family. He made his reputation breaking the monopoly which claimed that corn could only be ground in the parish where it was grown. The mill is shown in working condition, but having only two sails looks unusual. The date of this photograph can only be guessed at between 1880 and 1905, as the mill remained in commission for more than ninety years in the days when the island had to be more self-sufficient.

The mill is still very much in use. It was built from Guernsey pink granite and survived the Occupation unscathed. Carefully preserved by the Best family it is now, on the ground floor, the jewellery shop of Catherine Best.

Returning to La Rue Poudreuse. Shown above is the dwelling of Alfred Guerin, the man wearing the top hat. He was the father of Alice Rose featured on page 42. At one time the house was called 'The Elms'. The dog in the window is featured in other photographs in this book, such as on page 21 and page 34; the dates of these photographs allows us to date the photograph above to before 1900, and possibly as early as the 1880s. As a law agent, Alfred Guerin would have had many connections with people on the island as well as his own extensive family.

This house had a large garden at the rear. The removal of blanking board to an old chimney in the kitchen revealed the nineteenth-century cooking range complete with its tools of the time. A more recent view of the house is to the left. To continue the tour we should return to Grange Road.

On page 41 we were looking down Grange Road towards St Julian's. We are now at the junction with Doyle Road leading off to the left. The four-horse coach would be needed for the steep climb out of the town up St Julian's Avenue, which in 1880 was described as a new road. This, as now, was a busy thoroughfare if the condition of the road is any indication. Behind the coach is St Andrew's Church which was not mentioned in the 1880 guide. The large building on the left was the Guernsey High School for Boys which was founded in 1891. Boys were permitted a temperance drink at 1 p.m. by arrangement with the principal. Children aged between five and eight years of age paid £1.50 per term; between eight and eleven years, £2; and over eleven years £3.

The Grange boasts some of the most beautiful houses on the island that in large part are externally unchanged although many of them are now put to business rather than residential use. The house on this corner was once occupied by the Pay family who owned the jewellers shop in the town (see page 31).

Looking back up Grange Road from a little further down the hill, the gated entrance to Elizabeth College is on the right. Endowed by Queen Elizabeth in 1563 the college languished for centuries with few students until 1824 when a new charter was sought and granted the following year. When the present building was commenced Elizabeth College was to become a premier centre of learning. Many of the students went on to achieve great things. Major Herbert Wallace Le Patourel, born in Guernsey in 1916, was a member of the same extended family featured in this book. During his time at Elizabeth College he represented the college at shooting and hockey before leaving to pursue a career in banking. He was later awarded the Victoria Cross in the Second World War.

Comparing the two photographs it would seem that significant changes have occurred over the years, and about the only identifying mark is the building on the left beyond the low wall and possibly the tops of the pillars on the right. To the right of the modern photograph is the side entrance to Elizabeth College.

This photograph was taken in around 1891 and shows Cyril Edwyn Ozanne, a pupil at Elizabeth College, when he was about fourteen years old. He was a member of the cadet force that was a feeder for the Royal Guernsey Militia. This uniform is believed to be of the Militia as Elizabeth College does not recognise it. There were two Militias on the island: the Town and the Country. The Militia were enrolled to defend the island and were not permitted to serve abroad. However when the call came the Royal Guernsey Light Infantry was formed. This force was composed of Guernsey men who wished to volunteer in the 1914-18 war – in which they suffered very heavy casualties. This resulted in a serious shortage of manpower in the island, which took decades to recover.

The modern Elizabeth College maintains this tradition as this modern cadet on the steps at the side of the college demonstrates. The present building, says the 1880 guide, was erected at great cost and would not have met with the approval of Welby Pugin or Sir Gilbert Scott being more reminiscent of Horace Walpole's modern-mediaeval villa at Twickenham with its pie-crust battlements, its bold, plastered, unmeaning face too prominent to be overlooked. That sounds a very harsh judgement by the standards of today on a much-loved building.

Directly opposite the entrance to Elizabeth College is Bonamy House, built in 1820 by John Wilson who also built Elizabeth College and the nearby St James Church. He was a pupil of architect John Soam. The house was built for John Collings and his wife Mary Bonamy. It has thirty-five rooms. Hilary Gosselin, connected with the family, had been awarded Letters of Marque to enable him to attack the French on behalf of the Sovereign. Jean Allaire, another distant relative of the author, is said to have gone one better. He secured Letters of Marque from the French as well and was said to bring his French captures to Guernsey while he hid the proceeds from British captures on the island of Jethou, to which he had acquired use and subsequently bought. Not a good friend to many people, his behaviour was scorned but he became a very rich and powerful man. Catherine Ann Allaire Collings was Alice Rose Ozanne's mother-in-law and is one of his descendants.

The elegant extension on the first floor was added to the house in about 1895. The house is still occupied by the same Collings family that had it built, and the name of Bonamy is carried on by Mary's descendants.

Chapter 3

BEYOND THE TOWN

It has been seen throughout this book how important the horse-drawn vehicle has proved to be for both leisure and industrial purposes on the island. It persevered despite the other means of transport available, even in 1880 against such inventions as the steam tramway, of which Ward & Lock's 1880 guide states: 'This capital institution furnishes pleasant carriages, which, dragged by the snorting brisk little iron horse "warranted free from vice and warranted a good roadster," spins merrily along the margin of Belle Greve Bay' for a distance of three miles. But horses were by and large the most common means of getting from place to place, whether for the inhabitants or for the visitors.

The modern bus has replaced the horse and trap. It can easily be found near the Town Church and counts its horsepower by the hundreds. For those content to let others navigate the narrow roads, buses are plentiful and follow most of the roads that we shall have taken.

Moving away from the town we see something of the countryside and bays for which Guernsey is justly famous. From the Town Church travel along South Parade towards the brewery. Take the steep winding climb up the Val de Terres, taking the first left into Fort George. Following the road round and down to the left we come upon this glorious view across St Peter Port.

The distant headland is St Sampson but on a good day the island of Alderney can be seen on the far horizon. A number of points can now be identified from previous pictures in this book; letter A is the town church, B is Castle Pier, C is Albert Pier and D is St Julian's Pier. The growth of trees prevents us getting the panorama the earlier photographer achieved.

The island was always garrisoned with British troops as well as the Royal Guernsey Militia. Because of the temperate climate, regiments returning from India could sometimes be stationed here to acclimatize before they continued with their journey to mainland Britain. By the time this picture was taken in the 1880s, Castle Cornet had become too small for military purposes. In the distance is the old Doyle Monument, featured on the next page.

The old photograph was taken from the white Belvedere House which can be seen on the left as you look across the field in the modern photograph on page 54. This elegant house was built in the early nineteenth century to accommodate unmarried officers. Note part of the bank in the distance that shows on the old photograph can still be seen with a house built on it. The conversion of Fort George to its present use was allowed in the 1960s.

This is a very early photograph of Catherine Anne Allaire Collings (1826–1879). She was the sister of the Revd W. Collings the Seigneur of Sark. It is unusual in that it is in full colour. The process was called *Daguerreotype a l'huile*; an invention by A. Laloue. She married Richard James Ozanne, the Rector of St Peter Port, and was the mother-in-law of Alice Rose Ozanne.

The modern view shows Belvedere House (mentioned on the previous page) of which Catherine would no doubt have known but would have been unlikely to visit, unlike Bonamy House (seen on page 50) which she would have known very well indeed.

Leaving Fort George, continue along Fort Road and turn left into La Route des Blanches. A number of suggestions were made for this old photograph when it was published in the *Guernsey Press* some time ago. Someone said it was called the Iron Needle but could not remember where it was. Was it part of the original Doyle Monument? The guide of 1880 says 'a monument worthily erected to the memory of a most valuable administrator and an active and energetic man – the late sir John Doyle, Lieutenant Governor of Guernsey. The Column, ninety-six feet in height, is ascended by a spiral staircase. The view from the square gallery at the top is most extensive, the base of the column being at an elevation of four hundred feet above the level of the sea'.

Whether this is the correct location of the old photograph is now uncertain though the stonework and the shape of the base may be a clue. But the view is certainly worth the visit.

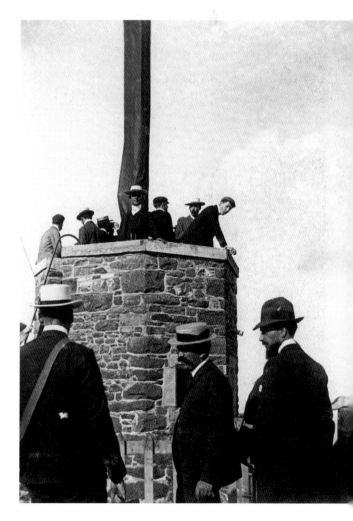

From here, if we return to the main road and branch off, we'll head for the Hotel Bon Port where permission should be sought to park in the hotel's car park. The steep walk down to Le Viet Port was immortalised by Pierre Auguste Renoir (1841-1919) who painted the bay eighteen times in 1833, some of these paintings can be seen in the Priaulx Library. The favoured time to arrive at the beach some way below is at low tide when the renowned rocks can be climbed and the Pea Stacks (off Jerbourg Point) can be viewed, as well as the excellent beach enjoyed. The top photograph shows Harold Hamilton, husband of Catherine Ozanne. An alternative approach is to walk from The Doyle Monument at Jerbourg Point.

This old photograph was taken along part of the coastal walk from Hotel Bon Port to Saints Bay. The stick that Catherine holds is called a cabbage stick and was a Channel Islands product. It was made by cutting and curing a plant of the cabbage family. In this photograph Catherine is wearing a wedding ring so it must have been taken after her marriage in 1907 to Harold Hamilton. By now Jean Le Patourel had died and the family was about to leave the island for England. This beautiful walk continues until it reaches the point where it branches left down to Saints Bay. Reproductions of the old-style benches as seen here are now beginning to appear.

The modern photograph reveals the cliff path has sunk a lot lower over time. This is a favourite walk for visitor and residents alike.

Returning now to the main road, and continuing on towards the airport, just as Le Chene Hill becomes Le Bourg you will find this row of cottages on the right. Repute has it that one was once occupied by a certain Thomas de la Rue who was world-renowned for his printing skills. The lady in the carriage is Alice Rose Ozanne, the mother of Catherine, whose husband was seen on the previous page. The date of the photograph above is between 1890 and 1900.

The modern photograph shows the same cottages behind the bus stop. The minimal changes prove the quality of the workmanship of the original builders. The lane behind you as you look at the cottages leads down to Petit Bôt Bay.

Continuing on the main road past the airport we turn left for Torteval and come to the district of St Pierre du Bois and the beginning of the North-West coast.

From the car park for Portelet Harbour can be seen the outside view of the Imperial Hotel's enclosed veranda. Here we have Catherine, aged about thirteen, in around 1894. Her mother Alice Rose Ozanne sits on her right. Behind is Alfred Guerin, the father of Alice Rose. He was a law agent; as a lawyer was termed in the island at that time. To his left is a family friend whose name is unknown but who appears elsewhere. Alice Rose's mother Elizabeth 'Eliza', the daughter of Jean Le Patourel, is behind the lady on the front right, who may be the second wife of Jean Le Patourel and who was known as 'the duchess'. This was obviously a very popular resort; the clothing in the image below indicates that people visited it at a different times of the year.

This modern view is of part of the Imperial's dining room where they were sitting. The ironwork was only recently removed having resisted the weather for 100 years. The original building constructed by John Groves & Son was the Weymouth Brewery. It is still described as 'new' in Guerin's Almanack of 1899 when the terms for lodging were 7 shillings (35p) per day. The owner in 1932 was Mr A.J. Dingle who sold it to the present owners; Randall's Brewery.

This house looks as though it is an early pre-fabricated structure. It is not known how many of these houses were built or where this one was in fact situated. The two little girls look happy enough with their cats and the woman behind watches the photographer resignedly. The seemingly suspended 'square' to the right may be the top of a heating chimney for the coal-fired boiler for one of the vineries. The greenhouses were originally built to produce grapes – hence the name.

An example of these unusual houses is to be found off La Rocquette near the golf course. The modern version looks a lot more comfortable than the early example.

Continuing along the coast road and passing the many fortifications on this coastal stretch, we arrive at Cobo Bay. On the right are the wooded slopes below Le Guet with its old Watch Tower. The road runs behind the seated girl in the old photograph. The beautiful Cobo Bay has often been painted by artists, including John Naftel in 1866, when the slope was exposed as in this photograph.

The modern photograph shows the slopes covered in woodland today. The road still curves round this granite outcrop. There is a car park at the base of the walk which leads up through the trees to where the ancient lookout can be visited. The view from the top is rewarding.

This watercolour dates from 1866 and shows the artists impression of Cobo Bay. It shows Le Guet with what appears to be a flagpole. Paul J. Naftel, the artist, was born on 10 September 1817 to a Guernsey family who originally came from Normandy. Entirely self-taught he began his career as an artist at the age of fourteen, and was to become Professor of Drawing at Elizabeth College. He was elected a full member of the Old Society of Painters in Water Colour in 1859. His paintings are much valued and examples are held in the Guernsey Museum at Candie Gardens. Naftel moved to London in 1870. His family is related to the Ozanne branch mentioned in this book. The church on the skyline is probably that of Castel which has very ancient connections and is set high up. A degree of artistic licence as to its visibility from this point should be allowed. The modern photograph does not give prominence to the church and the beach side cottages have gone – if in fact they ever existed.

Looking down from the Watch Tower across Cobo Bay, this old print was produced before the improved coastal road was completed. Possibly the pretty lane that takes the modern visitor up to the Watch Tower car park was available then. The famous Cobo beach in the lower photograph is sandy and on a clear day Alderney can be seen on the horizon to the right of the view.

Cobo is thought by many to be the most beautiful part of the island, and is loved as much by local people as it is by the visitor. A short walk from the lower car park for Le Guet brings you to this junction with La Route de Cobo. Here stands the little group of houses which are clearly visible in the two pictures on the previous page, and which appear to have changed very little in the last century. The horse bus stands before a wall that has needed little improvement in 100 years. We have seen the horseman before at the Arsenal, with the family at the Imperial.

Guerin's Almanac of 1899 states that the Picnic House was run by Mrs Foss and that 'Minibuses run hourly to and from town. Picnic Parties were supplied with Hot Water and Tea. Bread and Butter Teas and Aerated Water, which was readily available even in those days.

Amazingly this unknown group of Victorian young ladies sits amongst rocks that have once more disappeared below the sand. We were fortunate to just find the point of the rock behind the central figure. That point may well have vanished now if you try and find it by locating the position with the house behind, which has had two windows added in the roof during the intervening period.

The movement of sand in and out of Cobo Bay does not surprise local people who see it as part of the magical quality of the area. The sand is moved by storms that can lash this coast, and one severe winter storm can make a significant difference to the appearance of the beach. The huge tidal changes affect the water level so that small boats bravely moored in open water become surrounded by rocks when the tide falls.

This photograph dates from around 1897 when Cyril Ozanne, on the right, was about twenty years old. His grandfather, Alfred Guerin, is beside him, and his mother is behind on the left with his grandmother. Behind the family is the Rockmount Hotel. (also seen on page 63 when the hotel had no balcony).

Today the Rockmount Hotel has been adapted to its present shape. The sea wall has been raised and reinforced at beach level, probably when the road was improved, at which time it is possible that the stone steps were also replaced. One or two more houses have appeared and a building lost. The soft sand of the modern beach would surely have been preferred to the hard pebbles on which the Ozanne family sit. It is interesting to note that three generations of the same family all look very fit and well. Is it something in the Guernsey air?

This time-worn photograph shows two houses just beyond the Rockmount Hotel, which appear little changed today. The house on the right has changed its name from De Lecq to Lion Rock, named after a nearby feature. Magically, they seemed to have been able to stretch the garden to accommodate a car without moving the pillars. The shutters for the balcony have been replaced and a window reveals an attic conversion. As the level of the road appears to be the same as today, the old photograph must have been taken after the road was improved.

The house on the left appears to have had a chimney pot removed, the lower veranda closed in, and an extension on the side. Houses like these are a great credit to local builders, as winds can be extreme along this exposed coastline; the next land is the East American coast. These buildings can be seen in the background on pages 63 and 65.

A diversion down La Route de Cobo, turning left into La Rue Traversee and left into Ruette de la Tour will find the Ozanne Tower set back behind a bungalow on the right. This photograph was taken in 1897. The tower was built by Richard Mansell Ozanne in 1860. He was the grandfather of Richard Edwyn Ozanne, husband of Alice Rose Ozanne whose son Cyril is shown in the photograph. Richard James Ozanne, Alice's father-in-law sold the tower in 1873 to Joseph Freeman of Paddington and George Burt of Swanage for fifty-three quarters and two bushels of wheat. In 1938 it was sold by Lord De Saumarez to the island's water board. It was then sold in 2002 to the National Trust who intended to refurbish the tower. The Ozanne coat of arms appears over the door. During the war it was used as an observation post at which time the interior was changed.

Today the Ozanne Tower remains in reasonable structural repair – being constructed from durable Guernsey Granite – and the trees have been cut back so that it has good views out to sea – the function that it was originally designed for; that of a watch tower.

From this point we return to the coast road and continue on around the island before we divert inland to La Route de L'Islet at Grand Harbour.

Further along the Route de Cobo is Saumarez Park. This picture was thought to have been taken in around 1893 as Catherine is seen here aged about twelve years old. A previous owner of the Saumarez line built a set of features to reflect an interest in all things Japanese. Some still remain. The park is still open to the public now as it was then, though this bridge has gone.

Isabelle Mariess is standing on the modern bridge in the Japanese Garden. The tree behind looks similar to the one in the old picture.

Continuing along the coast road we arrive at the Grand Harbour area. Heading towards the Vale Parish Church, the other side of this pond can best be viewed from the bird watchers hide on the right-hand-side of the road. This pond and other similar areas going east across the island from Le Grand Havre to St Sampson are the remnants of the days when Guernsey was divided into two islands.

As one looks at these glimpses of Victorian life they seem a lot more relaxed and fun-loving than might be supposed. Or perhaps it is just the influence of Guernsey life on people.

This view of the pond is not readily accessible now as the area is very damp. The roof of the bird watching hide is on the left in the modern photograph. It may well have been part of the land that formed part of the Moncrieffe Vinery that was run by Harold and Catherine Hamilton for a period in the early 1900s.

This old map shows the original division of the two islands before they were combined by the simple expedient of filling in at Grand Harbour and closing off the other end at St Sampson. 'The Bridge' at St Sampson, which no longer exists, still echoes this. This work was completed in the early part of the nineteenth century and greatly aided the defence of the island against the French.

It can be seen from the modern photograph that in the past churchgoers would have rowed across to Vale Church from the other side of Braye de Vale and walked up the steps to enter the church grounds. At one time rings were visible in the sea wall, on the south side of the road, to which the boats would have been tied.

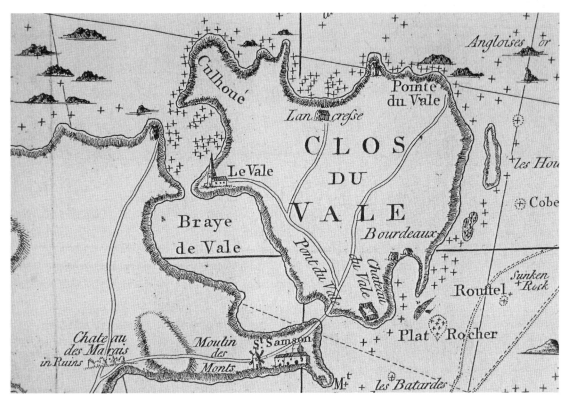

From Vale Church now divert down the Route Militaire. On your right was the old Moncrieffe Vinery. It is likely that this series of photographs were taken in around 1900. There is an optimism and pride in the Moncrieffe Vinery like many others at this time. Many were later to succumb to competitive strains, particularly from the Dutch, which were to cause their ultimate demise. Harold and Catherine would have worked together to make a success of it. In the top photograph, daffodils are being grown for the export trade. Behind, the Vale Church has changed very little.

The modern photograph shows the view today across the field towards Vale Church and the pond to the left.

Along La Route Militaire. The top of the house that can be seen above the greenhouses is still to be seen on the left in the modern photograph. On the other side of the road was the Moncrieffe Vineries that ran towards Vale Church. Harold Hamilton is carrying a bunch of lilies commercially grown for export.

All that remains of the Moncrieffe Vinery is the weed-covered brick foundations of some of the greenhouses. The use of greenhouses continues on the island today, so perhaps there are other reasons why this particular site was abandoned.

This old photograph was taken on 18 February 1899 by Harold Hamilton and shows that the Moncrieffe Vinery was far from new even at that time. An assistant is working in the greenhouse where the pipes for heating can also be seen. The boiler was usually at the end of the greenhouse and was brick built. Tall chimneys can still be seen around the island where old greenhouses are still in use. A problem now with these old style greenhouses is that the glass and other replacement parts are not as easily available as they were in the past. However some of the old greenhouses are still in use such as the one seen to the left belonging to David H. Falla at the Route des Capelles. It continues to produce beautiful blooms and hanging baskets all year round.

We now approach L'Ancresse Common at the northern extremity of the island; a place of ancient habitation long before the Christian period. In 1811 'Here, on the most elevated spot, is a cromlech or Druids' altar, of considerable dimensions' said Grigg's valuable Almanack; as reported by Ward & Lock's 1880 guide, which goes on to tell us that in 1837, through the enterprise and energetic efforts of local antiquary Dr Lukis, 'its hidden marvels were brought to light.' Races and other sports were once held on this pleasant spot. Here we see the preparations for the day's horse racing, which was often held on a Bank Holiday. Currently in use as a golf course, the racecourse, still shown on some maps, can be followed around the perimeter.

As we move on across the northern tip of the island the road curves inland away from the coast. In this area granite was quarried and boulders can still be seen at the side of the road. In this quieter, more relaxed period, a lady out for a drive could take time to pose for a photograph. Nowadays, although the roads do not seem wider they are certainly busier.

At Bordeaux Harbour turn left into Les Petils. There was a quarry on the left that has now been restored to a mound. Despite the fact that stone for the town church was imported from France much quarrying continued on the island. The Ward & Lock's 1880 guide says of the quarries:

'Here the work of getting the stone will be found proceeding in full activity. Very picturesque do these great stone pits appear, with their toiling occupants, who work like Titans, splitting up the great blocks and carting them away to the ships in the harbour.'

Along Les Petils these two ringed concrete blocks can be found on the right of the beach. Perhaps the old crane, called a Blondin, rested here when the quarry was working.

L eaving Bordeaux we continue on to St Sampson. Passing 'The Bridge', which has not been a bridge for nearly 200 years, we can enjoy the broad curve of Belle Greve Bay, dramatically different at high and low tide, there is an interesting corner called La Salerie, on Salt Street, where salt was once collected. The name goes back to an era when it was not unknown for payment, or salary, to be made in salt for work done.

It is not known where the bear originated, although it seems completely relaxed with the world around him (or her), and has drawn quite a crowd. Although on a lead the bear would take some holding if he decided he wished to be elsewhere.

Sadly the modern scene has lost some of its charm, but it is clear to see that although some things have been added to the area little has been removed. The cobbled area still lies beneath the tarmac.

This second photograph in the same area again shows the trust the people had in the good nature of the bear. It is unlikely that the bear belonged on the island as, with the small population, the novelty would not last for long. The imagination conjures with the prospect of the animal arriving by ferry. Would this seemingly benevolent creature travel in a cage or perhaps be allocated a cabin where he could rest with dignity whilst he prepared himself for his adoring public. Small children, even some in prams, are completely unrestrained. Modern legislation would make such scenes totally prohibited now.

The modern photograph shows the same area today largely taken up by car parking spaces. The sea wall identifies the location.

Leaving Salerie we continue into town until we reach St Julian's Pier and find ourselves back where we started. The tour has given you an opportunity to see parts of the island you might otherwise have missed. Perhaps the most surprising thing is that the island has changed so little. We still have a number of photographs of places that do seem to have changed, or in some cases disappeared.

Initially we were unable to locate this picture as St Julian's Pier looks so different now. The steps have gone and the wall before the town has changed. The trees have grown up around the Victoria Tower, but the roofs of the buildings along the North Esplanade can readily be identified. The modern photograph was taken from Cambridge Berth looking towards the town.

Chapter 4

PEOPLE, PLACES AND PUZZLES

It has been suggested that the occasion in this photograph is the Golden Jubilee Parade for Queen Victoria in 1887. Was it on the flats of L'Ancresse Common? This is possible as behind is what could be St Sampson view from L'Ancresse. The Argyle and Southerland Highlanders were stationed on the island for four years. This must have been an important occasion as the Highlanders are formally dressed, complete with their Feathered Bonnets (not Busbies). The Royal Guernsey Militia would also have been present.

It should always be remembered that the position occupied by the Channel Islands is unique. It is said that whereas Jersey was peopled by Brittany folk, Guernsey was peopled by Normandy folk. The rivalry has always been intense but this did not stop the regular inter-marriage of families between the two islands. The Guernsey cartoonist Guppy revelled in this rivalry. Ask a native of Guernsey when they became independent of mainland Britain and he will patiently explain. William the Conqueror was a Norman and also Duke of Normandy. Guernsey was part of that Dukedom.

La Route du Landes. Le Landes is a common name and in the case of this family indicates a property that had been in the family since 1576. The family once also owned Le Friquet, now a hotel, as a private residence. Next to it was this farm called Le Landes. Although this farm only extended to about thirty acres, such was the fertility of the soil that in the past it was prosperous. Sadly all that remains of the house now is a lintel that rests in the garden of a member of the Ozanne family. For those interested, Charles Ozanne has written a comprehensive history of the Ozanne family.

The last family owner of the house was Richard Collings Ozanne (1873-1956), eldest son of Alice Rose who sold the property in 1910 to the tenants, a family by the name of Sherwill. Ambrose Sherwill a popular Bailiff of Guernsey was born there in around 1880. Richard Collings Ozanne emigrated to Canada when the property was sold. The stone has cut into it 'POZ 1764' which refers to Pierre Ozanne (1741-1823) who inherited the property at this time.

It would be wrong to think that the horse is no longer a popular means of transport. Riding establishments abound on the island where visitor and resident alike can enjoy the delight so obviously expressed by this unknown young man from the turn of the twentieth century.

Particular thanks are due to Sofia, her father and Pineapple the pony, not to mention their dog, of La Carriere Stables and Tack Shop.

In the past, animals were much more involved in the daily lives of people than they are today; then they were needed for both food and transport. The island was often cut off for considerable periods by the weather and sometimes the forces of war, so people had to be able to obtain all their needs from the island itself. *The Book of Ebenezer Le Page* by the late G.B. Edwards provides a good description of daily life in Guernsey during the first half of the twentieth century.

Particular thanks for the smaller photograph are due to Pam and Tom de Garis, their daughter and grandchildren, who gave their time and patience in making the modern photographic equivalent to the old photograph look so easy.

Then of course there was always the bicycle. From this photograph it is reasonable to deduce that the roads must have been quite good. After all on a small island with a substantial population the road would get much use and this is proved by all the evidence of vehicles in this book. Of course for the young a bicycle would do. It did not need to be fed or tended and in the context of comparison with the horse it must have been the transport which every young man craved. Cyril Ozanne, brother of Catherine, is pictured aged about twenty here in 1897, and is obviously very proud of his.

Along with the updated and popular mode of transportation, the modern photograph at Albert Pier also shows the commemorative plaque of the visit of the Duke of Connaught in 1905, also featured earlier in this book.

Page 9 showed the ring where we are supposed to tie up on on our arrival. This ring can be found in the little alley which runs up from The Quay to Le Pollet oppiosite Crown Pier, also called Victoria Pier. It has been suggested that it was used to tie a horse. Or did they mean a hawse for a small boat? Many people believe that this alleyway is actually the old slope down to the waterside used long before the Victorian extensions we see today were constructed.

The Royal Channel Island Yacht Club has been established in Guernsey for about fifty years. It took over from the older club in Jersey which dates from the nineteenth century

This vessel may well have been a collier, bringing coal from wherever it could be cheaply purchased to sell at the best price on the island. It is impossible to over-estimate the skill and seamanship of the skipper and crew of ships like this. Trusting only to the wind and tide they were often at the mercy of fast-moving currents which could carry a vessel onward at more than twelve miles an hour. The date of this picture is unknown but it must be in the latter part of the nineteenth century as even the ferry in the background appears to be less modern than those seen earlier in the book and may even have been powered by paddle wheels.

This modern Guernsey vessel, the *Revelation II*, is the creation of Mr Jim Wilkinson and would have been a revelation to the skippers of the past.

Where have all these people on the boat shown on the left come from, and where are they going? Intriguingly, in the background, they seem to have managed to lift a very substantial vessel onto the dockside. The strongest possibility for its location is on Castle Pier as there would be plenty of room for the vessel. There was a floating dock on the island at about this time. No reference can be found to The Liquid Fuel Engineering Co.

The oarsmen in the early photograph would no doubt have welcomed the engine of the modern rigid inflatable boat seen in the modern photograph below but where the Liquid Fuel Co. would have been able to help is not known

This vessel (with the benefit of digital enhancement) has the name *Nordsea* written on its side, just above the small boat, and on both the funnels is what appears to be a red cross, while on the stern is a flag which cannot be identified except to say that it is not French. Several of the vessels seem to be flying the same flag. Considerable interest is apparent by the crowd on the buttress. The date is uncertain but the subject is more likely to be of interest to Harold Hamilton who is known to have taken some of the photographs in this book, therefore the date must again be at the turn of the twentieth century. It seems extraordinary also that these vessels should be moored in the mouth of the harbour.

Leaving the harbour this modern yacht sails through the same area and gives some idea of the considerable size of the vessels. Both views are from the walkway at the end of White Rock Pier.

Here is another photograph of these intriguing mystery vessels. They are moored outside the harbour or it would not be possible to photograph them with the wall in the foreground. The island of Sark lies behind. Presumably the hanging bell-like items are lights. There is a lot of interest in the vessels by the little boats all around them.

This Condor ferry is passing the island of Sark as it approaches St Peter Port from Jersey.

The mystery continues. The same vessels are now moored in the middle of the harbour. They do not have the look of steam vessels as they have no funnel. They may be sailing vessels which for some reason have had their rigging removed. Whatever they were and whatever they were doing, they seem to be waiting out in the middle of the Port.

The modern photograph shows the same two points of White Rocks Pier and the end of Castle Pier. The 'new' Jetty can be seen before White Rocks Pier. Yachts arriving at St Peter Port have to wait until the tide is up sufficiently for them to enter the marinas which are protected by bars to keep a level of water within, meanwhile they must wait at one of these pontoons.

This view, probably taken from the top of the Victoria Tower, contrasts with the modern photograph taken from the same location in 1999, when access to the Victoria Tower was still permitted. It is hoped that one day the Victoria Tower will again be open to the public, so that they may benefit from the glorious views from the top. Because of the technical changes with modern cameras there is a far greater range of field available now.

The Candie cemetery, which lies between Candie Gardens and Monument Road, still provides a haven of calm. It is the cemetery for the Town Church of St Peter on the sea front. Some island families still retain access to family plots.

This view of the Candie Gardens shows a concert at the bandstand on a clear and beautiful summer day, when the islands of Herm and Sark can be seen on the horizon. The bandstand is still to be seen as part of the Guernsey Museum complex.

This view today was taken from the second floor of the Priaulx Library and shows that Queen Victoria has lost her view across the harbour. The roofs in the middle are those of the Museum.

Then suddenly it is all over. Queen Victoria is dead and an empire mourns. None more so than the people of Guernsey. During her reign, as has been seen, huge sums were invested in the island. Great building works completed to make the island ready for the twentieth century. Her statue in Candie Gardens was only a year old when dressed to mourn her passing. How well people saw into the future can be judged by how well Guernsey adapts and how little has changed.

This modern photograph was taken on an April day when the island races forward into the spring of another year. Perhaps it is best to think of Guernsey with its French names and very much with its own unique personality as: 'Not quite England but no longer France.'

Catherine is sat here on a mooring post at the end of Albert Pier. Behind her is the end of White Rock Pier. The photograph might well have been taken towards the time she left for England with her husband Harold, probably around 1910 or 1911. First, they went to Portsmouth where they lived while Harold tried to become established. He aspired to be a photographer and may well have taken most of the photographs in this book. After going to England they had two daughters, Daphne May, who was born in 1909, and Eileen Maie in 1911. Harold lost his life in the First World War in 1918.

The interception of the wall of the modern photograph behind the author is at Fish Quay (see page 22).

It is again interesting to see how little this point has changed. The holes made by the Victorian metal railing can still be seen in the stone of the quay wall. It has been said that temporary buildings were placed at this point during the Second World War but these have now been removed.

Other local titles published by Tempus

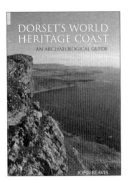

Dorset's World Heritage Coast An Archaeological Guide
JOHN BEAVIS

This exploration of the Dorset coast from Studland to Lyme Regis shows the reader how to recognise and interpret traces of past human activity. Every period from the late Stone Age to the present is represented, and almost all types of archaeological sites are encountered in the book. A section of the guide groups the sites in chronological order and provides a summary of the most important historical changes they illustrate.
0 7524 2545 5

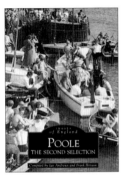

Poole The Second Selection
ALAN ANDREWS AND FRANK HENSON

This book contains over 200 scenes from all aspects of life in Poole over the years. Once familiar buildings, shops and firms are recalled, and people are seen involved in all manner of work and play activities. There is an interesting feature about Poole Town Football Club and another about Poole lifeboats. Schools, hospitals, pubs, churches and carnivals all make an appearance.
0 7524 1624 3

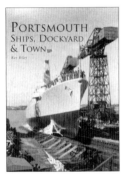

Portsmouth Ships, Dockyard & Town
RAY RILEY

For a long time Portsmouth has been known as a Dockyard town, and indeed until the 1980s, when the last great contraction of the yard took place, this was certainly the case. With over 200 images of the town's largest employers including the Dockyard, and its associated industries – including commercial shipbuilding and engineering – in the town, they show a changed way of life that will never be replaced.
0 7524 2776 8

Southampton The Second Selection
A.G.K. LEONARD

This compilation of over 220 photographs and other images document the many aspects of social history and development of Southampton from Victorian times to the Second World War. They recall bygone townscapes, transport and shipping scenes, past occupations, occasions and recreations, and some of the people who made their distinctive contributions to the growth of the town and port.
0 7524 2484 X

If you are interested in purchasing other books published by Tempus, or in case you have difficulty finding any Tempus books in your local bookshop, you can also place orders directly through our website

www.tempus-publishing.com